Tr[...]l in School

Written by Helen Comerford
Illustrated by Scott Brown

HODDER Education

Hachette UK's policy is to use papers that are natural, renewable and recyclable products and made from wood grown in well-managed forests and other controlled sources. The logging and manufacturing processes are expected to conform to the environmental regulations of the country of origin.

ISBN: 978 1 3983 7733 2

Text © Helen Comerford
Design, illustrations and layout © Hodder & Stoughton Limited
First published in 2023 by Hodder Education,
An Hachette UK Company
Carmelite House, 50 Victoria Embankment, London EC4Y 0DZ
www.hoddereducation.com

Impression number 10 9 8 7 6 5 4 3 2 1
Year 2027 2026 2025 2024 2023

Author: Helen Comerford
Series Editor: Catherine Coe
Commissioning Editor: Hamish Baxter
Illustrator: Scott Brown/Bright Group International
Educational Reviewer: Pauline Allen
Page layouts: Rocket Design (East Anglia) Ltd
Editorial: Amy Tyrer

With thanks to the schools that took part in the development of *Reading Planet* KS2, including: Ancaster CE Primary School, Ancaster; Downsway Primary School, Reading; Ferry Lane Primary School, London; Foxborough Primary School, Slough; Griffin Park Primary School, Blackburn; St Barnabas CE First & Middle School, Pershore; Tranmoor Primary School, Doncaster; and Wilton CE Primary School, Wilton.

The publishers would like to thank the following for permission to reproduce copyright material: pp8, 10-13 © ~ Bitter ~/stock.adobe.com; pp16-19, 25-26 © D&R studio/stock.adobe.com; p29, 32, 36 © Alwi/stock.adobe.com; pp39, 43-46, 51-53 © Nata_Smilyk ゾ/stock.adobe.com

A catalogue record for this title is available from the British Library.

Printed in the UK.

Orders: Please contact Hachette UK Distribution, Hely Hutchinson Centre, Milton Road, Didcot, Oxfordshire, OX11 7HH.
Telephone: +44 (0)1235 400555. Email: primary@hachette.co.uk

MIX
Paper | Supporting
responsible forestry
FSC
www.fsc.org   FSC™ C104740

Contents

ACT IT OUT!

Character list

Naya

Ashwin

Jo

Eddie

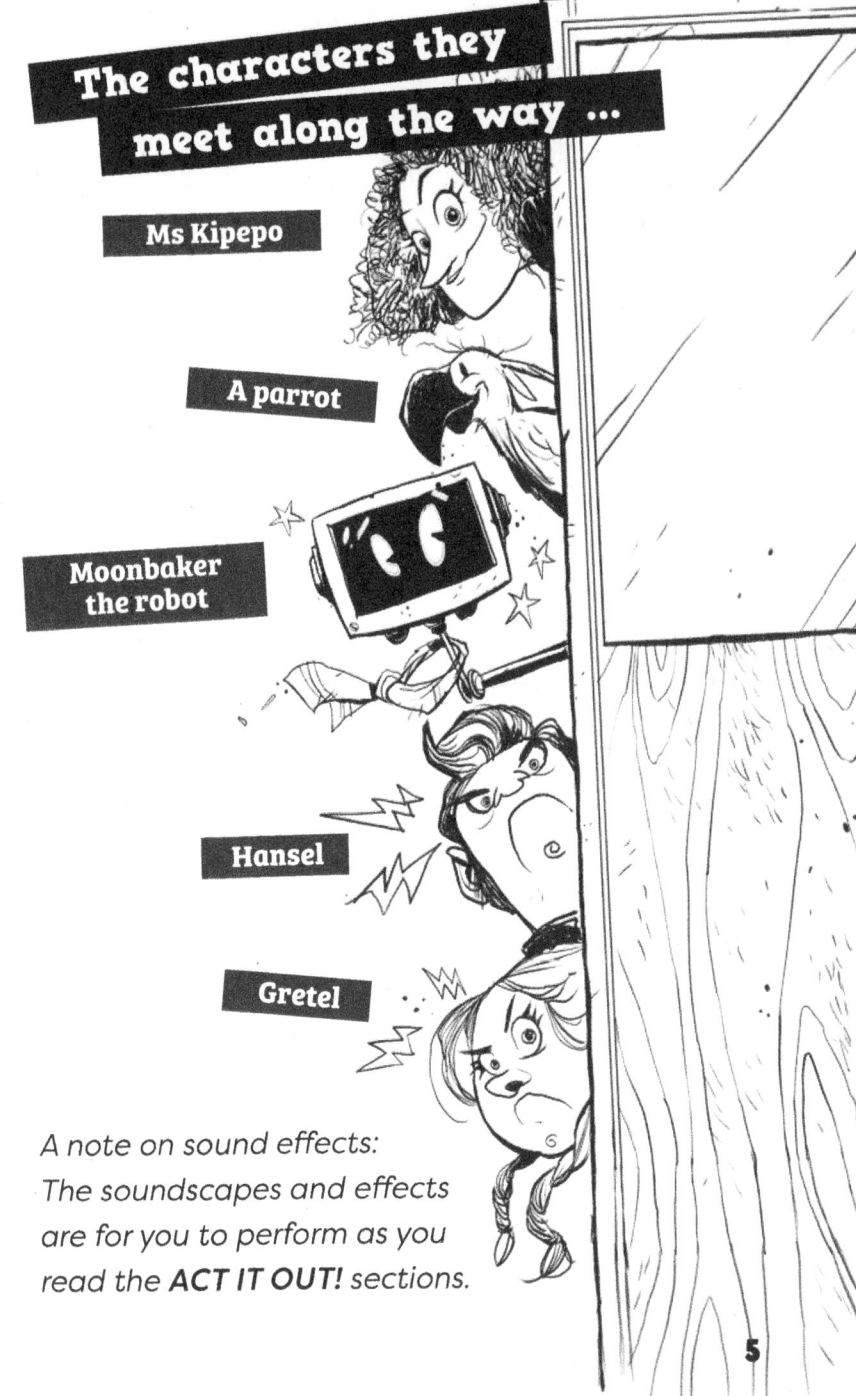

The characters they meet along the way ...

Ms Kipepo

A parrot

Moonbaker the robot

Hansel

Gretel

A note on sound effects:
The soundscapes and effects
are for you to perform as you
*read the **ACT IT OUT!** sections.*

5

1 Welcome to Lonely Grove

There are more types of magic in this world than there are leaves in a forest, and the magic of Lonely Grove Primary School was one of a kind. Perched on the top of a hill, overlooking the town below, Lonely Grove Primary seemed like an ordinary building. It was an ordinary school, built around an ordinary grove of silvery trees, which glimmered in a very ordinary way in the sunshine.

Neither the teachers nor the children knew that their school was magic, but the school didn't mind. It was happy waiting.

Naya didn't know about the magic. She knew about the terrifying spiders that scuttled out of dark corners in the toilets, and the swings in the playground that went too high, and the whistling wind in the assembly hall that sounded like a ghost and made her heart hammer. That was all frightening enough.

The clock was hidden by vines from the class jungle display, but home time was so close that Naya could almost taste it. As soon as class finished, she planned to head straight back to her house and remain there – safe, secure and slightly bored, until she had to come to school again.

"Who can tell me what kind of trees are in our grove?" Mr McGregor asked.

"I know." Ashwin, Naya's best friend, flapped his hand in the air. "I know ... I know!"

"Yes, Ashwin?" Mr McGregor said.

"The answer is ..." Ashwin hummed, "... silver birch trees."

"Very good, Ashwin."

"And they're deciduous," Ashwin continued.

"Excellent, Ashwin."

"And they release pollen between March and May."

"Okay, Ashwin, thank you." Mr McGregor held up his hands. "That's us finished for today. Make sure you leave your tables nice and tidy."

ACT IT OUT!

It's the end of the day at Lonely Grove Primary School and Class 4M chat whilst they pack their bags.

Ashwin: We should stop at the park on the way home!

Naya: Or we could go somewhere nice and quiet and read a book?

Ashwin: Or we could stop in the woods and search for some interesting insects!

Jo comes to join Ashwin and Naya.

Jo: I'll come and find insects!

Ashwin: Yay!

Jo: Oh wait. *(Jo sighs.)* I've got instructions from Mum to get Eddie from Reception, take him straight home and hold his hand the whole way.

Ashwin: I know! We can go through the woods to your house and your brother can come too! Naya can hold his hand whilst we search for green huntsmen. She's terrified of even the most miniscule spiders.

Naya: I'm not!

Ashwin and Jo: You are!

Ashwin: Come on. Let's find Eddie.

Naya, Ashwin and Jo headed out into the corridor and past the star on the door of Class 5K. Naya had snuck into 5K earlier to look at their display about the moon, and shivered as she gazed up at the stars dangling from the ceiling. If the display was supposed to teach her that space was intimidating, endless and freezing cold, then it had done its job perfectly.

A stampede of five-year-olds thundered past as the trio reached Reception and paused by the classroom door. It had been decorated to look like gingerbread, which was a display that Naya approved of. What could be frightening about fairytales?

"Come on, Eddie!" Jo shouted into Reception.

ACT IT OUT!

Ashwin, Naya and Jo peer into Reception.

Jo: Eddie?

Naya: He's disappeared.

Ashwin: Let's ask a teacher.

Ms Kipepo appears.

Ashwin: Ms Kipepo, where's Eddie?

Ms Kipepo: Are you coming, Eddie? You're the last one again! Are you walking him home, Jo?

Jo: Yes, Ms Kipepo.

Eddie wanders out slowly, holding his shoes.

Eddie: Hi, Jo!

Ms Kipepo: Lovely. See you tomorrow!

Ms Kipepo rushes off.

Jo: *(Annoyed)* Where were you? We were waiting.

Eddie: I was sitting by the pegs. My laces came undone. Can you help me, Jo?

Jo: You're such a baby.

Naya: I'll help you, Eddie.

Naya patiently assists Eddie with his shoes.

Eddie: Thanks, Naya.

Jo: Are you finally ready, Eddie?

Ashwin: Come on, team. Let's go to the woods.

Naya: When did it get so quiet? Has everyone left school already?

The children head towards the front door.

Jo: Yes! Because baby Eddie made us late.

Eddie: Sorry, Jo.

Ashwin: Never mind. The insects will still be slithering and scuttling when we get to the woods.

Naya: Yuck.

Ashwin pushes the front door.

Ashwin: What's wrong with the door? It won't budge.

Naya: The door won't open?

Jo: Let me try. *(Jo bashes into the door.)* Argh!

Naya: *(Louder)* The door won't open?!

Ashwin: I know ... you're turning the handle the wrong way. *(He tries again.)* Nope. It won't open.

Naya: *(Shouts)* The door won't open?!

Jo: Don't be frightened, Naya.

Naya: Don't tell me not to be frightened. *(Naya tugs on the door handle.)* We're trapped in school!

2 Ashwin's Plan

The way out of Lonely Grove Primary was locked. No matter how much they heaved, shoved or wiggled the door, it wouldn't budge. They were trapped.

Ashwin's heart beat faster and he gritted his teeth. His mind was whirring – he knew that this was a problem that only he could solve. Sparkles hung around the children in the dim corridor as Ashwin set out his plan.

ACT IT OUT!

Ashwin: Okay, listen up, everybody. This is bad and I know you are frightened ...

Jo: I'm not frightened. It's Naya who's the scaredy cat.

Naya: I am not!

Ashwin: ... but it's going to be completely fine ... No, it's going to be absolutely excellent. I know what to do. I'm going to get us all home in time for tea.

Naya: How?

Eddie: Ashwin, there's—

Jo: Shhh, Eddie!

Ashwin: Step one: we get some rope from the gym. Step two: we climb on to the roof and lasso a tree. *(Ashwin pretends to lasso.)* Step three: we tie the other end of the rope to the roof and zipline to safety. *(Ashwin grins triumphantly.)*

Jo: I have some questions. What are we using to slide down the rope? How do we get on the roof?

Naya: How do we not fall off the roof and break our legs?

Ashwin: The plan isn't perfect, but I'll solve all those problems as we go.

Naya: Like us falling off the roof and breaking our legs?

Jo: It's a terrible plan, Ashwin.

Eddie: But Jo, there's a—

Jo: Shhh, Eddie!

Ashwin: I know ... new plan! We go out of the fire exit in our classroom.

Naya: Okay, excellent idea. Let's do that.

As the children rushed back towards Class 4M, the sunlight shining in through the windows seemed to fade, and the electric lights that ran along the ceiling dimmed to a soft glow. The gloomy corridor filled with shadows.

"It's still daytime, isn't it?" Naya asked, but no one knew what to say.

During the school day, there was normally the sound of maths, reading, or music coming out of Class 4M. But now, Ashwin could hear a strange noise that was like a whoosh, a rustle and a rumble all squashed together.

"That doesn't sound right." Naya crept closer to the door. "I don't know if we should go in there."

"It's just the wind." Ashwin marched past. He wasn't about to let some random rumbling slow them down. "Come on. The fire exit is just on the other side of our nice, normal, safe classroom."

Ashwin swung the door open and the children followed him inside. It was as dark as the corridor at first, and then the lights came back on so ferociously that Ashwin blinked spots away from his eyes.

He couldn't make sense of the dazzling, green light, or the stifling heat. They were surrounded by a cacophony of sounds – rustles, squawks, creaks and noises he couldn't recognise. What was going on?

"This isn't our classroom," Jo said, slowly.

"It's a jungle!" Eddie cried.

The children turned back to the door in time to see it slam shut, shimmer and fade out of existence.

Jungle Soundscape

What sounds would Ashwin, Naya, Jo and Eddie hear in the jungle?

Make some jungle sound effects. If there's a group of you acting the story out, you could choose one each:

- **A rushing waterfall**
- **Squawking parrots**
- **Laughing monkeys**
- **A growling jaguar**
- **Croaking tree frogs**
- **A screaming eagle**
- **A clicking insect**

If you're working as a group, make your sounds together to create a soundscape.

- **Try it softly**
- **Try it loudly**
- **Try with some sounds loud and some soft**

Play with your soundscape to see what you like and look out for the sound effects in the **ACT IT OUT!** sections.

The children stared at the place where the door used to be. Around them, enormous trunks twisted up to fill the sky with wide green leaves. A dangling vine brushed Ashwin's shoulder, and below his feet a carpet of leaves rustled like there were hundreds of insects, busy underneath. Another time, Ashwin would have stopped to study them, but this was not the time for insects. This was the time for action.

ACT IT OUT!

The sounds of the jungle come alive around the children.

Sound effect: Loud jungle soundscape, which fades slowly out

Naya: *(Quietly)* We're in a jungle.

Ashwin: This might look bad, but I'm certain I'll be able to get us home.

Naya: *(Louder)* We're in a jungle.

Eddie: Is it magic, Jo?

Jo: I don't know.

Naya: *(Shouts)* We're in a jungle!

Ashwin: I know! Maybe the door just moved. Let's find it.

The children search frantically.

Jo: This is useless! We all saw the door disappear. There are just leaves and vines and …

Sound effect: Monkeys laugh

Jo: *(Whispers)* … wild animals.

Ashwin: Come on! This way!

The children run one way.

Sound effect: A growling jaguar

The children rush back.

Jo: Not that way.

Eddie: Jo, look—

Jo: Shhh, Eddie.

Ashwin: I know … it's this way.

The children run another way.

Sound effect: Laughing monkeys

The children dart back.

Naya: Did you see the whiteboard? It was up in one of the trees and had a picture of the silver trees from our school on it.

Jo: No, but I saw a desk sticking out of some ferns.

Ashwin: I saw some chairs tangled up in the vines. Let's go back and look again.

The children creep back towards the monkeys.

Eddie: Look over there!

Ashwin: What is it, Eddie? What's that glowing green box? Oh, I know, it's the fire exit sign. Quick!

The children race after Ashwin.

Sound effect: *(Quiet)* **Rushing waterfall**

Naya: What's that noise?

Jo: It sounds like water.

Sound effect: *(Louder)* **Rushing waterfall**

Naya: No, that's not just water.

Ashwin: It's coming from the other side of those trees.

The children push through the trees.

Sound effect: *(Loudest)* **Rushing waterfall**

Naya: It's a waterfall, Ashwin! And the fire exit is on the other side.

3 The Jungle

The waterfall cascaded over a cliff and into a deep turquoise pool below. Scarlet macaws swooped in and out of the mist, before landing back on the trees that lined a loopy path down the hillside. Jo's cheeks grew hot and she scowled. If it hadn't been for Eddie, they'd all be home by now and not lost in some stupid jungle.

Jo edged closer to the rushing river and tried to see where the fire exit door was, but only the glowing sign was visible behind the hanging vines.

"I know." Ashwin pointed back up the river. "Look! There are some stepping stones over the water. Let's cross there. We'll be out of this jungle and home in no time."

Jo followed Ashwin's finger to five stones that protruded from the white, frothing river. Her heart gave a painful thump, and she bit her lip. The stones barely looked wide enough to stand on, and the middle one was covered in slippery-looking green weeds. It was a long way between each stone, and, if they fell, it was even further down the waterfall and into the pool below.

"That's a terrible idea." Naya pointed in the opposite direction, towards the hillside. "Look, we can walk down to the pool, go around the waterfall and get back up the other side."

Jo's eyes tracked the trail down through the mess of trees and giant leaves, out around the pool and up what looked like a thousand steps up in the direction of the fire exit. It made her feet ache just looking at it.

"My way is quicker," Ashwin said.

"We don't always have to do things your way." Naya stamped her foot.

"It's okay, Naya," Eddie called from behind them. "I'll go first."

Jo whipped her head round and her heart stopped. Eddie was already on the first stone. "Stop, Eddie! They're too far apart for you," Jo cried.

"Eddie, come back!" Naya yelled.

"Don't worry!" Eddie swung his arms, once, twice, three times and leapt. Jo could hardly bear to watch as her little brother landed on the second stone.

"See," Eddie said. "I can do it!"

Jo shook her head. The gap to the next stone was even bigger. "That's great. You showed us. Just come back now," she called, over the roar of the waterfall. "That middle stone looks slippery."

Eddie didn't listen. He swung his arms, once, twice, three times and leapt.

"No!" shouted Jo.

For a moment it looked like Eddie was going to land safely on the middle stone. His front foot reached the green surface, but with a whoosh it slipped off, and with a splash Eddie tumbled into the water.

"Eddie!" Jo rushed over to the river and on to the first stone and then the next. "Eddie?" The roar of the waterfall was even louder near the middle of the river. Jo crouched on the stone. She couldn't see him.

"Oh, no!" cried Naya.

Jo looked at where the torrent of water thundered over the edge, just in time to see Eddie hurtle over it.

"Eddie," she whispered.

"This is your fault!" Naya yelled at Ashwin.

"It doesn't matter whose fault it is!" Jo snapped.

The children peered over the treetops at the turquoise pool far below. "Please be okay," Jo whispered. "Please be okay, Eddie." There was no sign of him. She should have held his hand, just like Mum said.

"Look!" Naya pointed down, and there was Eddie doggy paddling to the edge of the pool.

As Eddie pulled himself out of the water and lay panting on the shore, relief washed over Jo and she blinked back tears. Her brother was safe.

ACT IT OUT!

Sound effect: Loud rushing waterfall, fades out slowly

Jo: Quick! We need to get down there to rescue him. Follow me!

Sound effect: A parrot squawks

The children battle through the branches on the trail, down to the pool.

Ashwin: It wasn't my fault.

Naya: It was. You never listen, Ashwin – we always have to do your plan, even when it's ridiculous.

Parrot: Squawk! Ridiculous!

Ashwin: It's not my fault I'm the one who has the fun ideas. If it was up to you, we'd just hide in our bedrooms all day, every day, because you're a scaredy cat.

Parrot: Squawk! Scaredy cat!

Jo: Stop arguing. We need to find Eddie.

Naya: You didn't even care about your brother until he fell over a waterfall, Jo!

Parrot: Squawk! Jo!

Jo: Eddie? He sounds strange. Is that an echo or—

Parrot: Jo!

Jo:　　Eddie! Quick, he's this way.

Jo rushes off the trail.

Ashwin:　Jo, wait!

Jo hurtles through the branches and vines with Ashwin and Naya close behind.

Jo:　　Eddie?

Parrot:　Jo!

Jo:　　Eddie, I'm coming!

Parrot:　Scaredy cat.

Jo:　　What?

Parrot:　Ridiculous.

Sound effect: Loud rushing waterfall, fades out slowly

Naya:　　Jo, wait – that's not Eddie.

Ashwin:　It's a parrot, Jo. They can mimic human voices. Some parrots, like the African grey, can learn hundreds of words.

Parrot:　Squawk! Ridiculous!

Jo:　　Oh, no! *(Jo starts to cry.)* I'm so silly!

Naya:　　It's okay, Jo, we're not far from the trail. We'll be down at the pool soon.

Jo:　　He's too little to be in a terrifying jungle on his own. I should have held his hand. We need to find him.

Parrot:　Squawk! Find him.

4 Behind the Waterfall

Jo, Ashwin and Naya pushed back through the branches to the rocky trail that snaked down the hillside. It didn't take them long to reach the pool at the bottom of the waterfall, but Eddie was nowhere to be seen.

"Where could he have gone?" Jo cried. She clenched her fists tightly by her side. Eddie should have waited for her to come and find him. "Eddie!"

"I know ..." Ashwin clapped his hands and a flock of parrots took off from a nearby tree. "... Reconnaissance! Let's split up and search. He can't have gone far."

Jo didn't waste time arguing. She leapt over a mass of honey-scented yellow flowers, and hurtled down a path, calling her brother's name. She had to find him. Jo hadn't made it far through the ferns when a cry from Naya floated through the air.

"Come back!"

A breathless Jo crashed back into the clearing. Naya and Ashwin were waiting for her by the waterfall, looking damp, but excited.

Jo rushed round to join them. Up close, the thundering water was so loud it felt like it was shaking her bones. Naya beckoned Jo closer and pointed through the torrent. Beyond the wall of water were the dark wet rocks of the hillside and something that shone silver in the gloom. Two vertical silver lines with another silver line across the top.

"It's a door!" Jo yelled, and stepped through the pouring water into the cave beyond.

"Oh! I'm soaked!" Naya joined her, shaking the water from her hair. "Where do you think it leads?"

The door looked just like the door to their classroom, except that it was in a dark wet cave in a jungle.

Ashwin crept closer. "It sounds quiet," he said. "Maybe it leads back to the corridor?"

Jo's fingers closed around the handle. "It must be where Eddie went, so it's where I'm going, too." She flung open the door.

Beep. Beep. Beep.

Tiny lights were flashing. Tiny beeps were beeping. And through the window there was a rocky, grey desert under a blanket of stars. There was no doubt about it – they were on a spaceship on the moon.

Space Soundscape

What sounds would Ashwin, Naya and Jo hear on the spaceship?

Make some space sound effects. If there's a group of you acting the story out, you could choose one each:

- **Beeping equipment**
- **A passing asteroid**
- **An airlock opening and closing**
- **An alarm**
- **The computer giving information**
- **The rumbling engine**
- **Some clicking equipment**

If you're working as a group, make your sounds together to create a soundscape.

- **Try it softly**
- **Try it loudly**
- **Try with some sounds loud and some soft**

Play with your soundscape to see what you like and look out for the sound effects in the *ACT IT OUT!* sections.

Jo didn't turn around as the door slammed shut behind them. "Eddie?" she whispered.

She rushed around the wide control room. Beneath the window there was a long console of flashing buttons. Some spacesuits hung by a sign that said 'Airlock' and panels with lights covered the walls.

"He's not here." Jo's shoulders sagged. The door to the jungle was gone. If Eddie wasn't on the spaceship, then maybe she really had lost him.

"Pssssht!" The sound came from the radio. "Min, could you bring the buggy round to the east side of the crater?"

"Pssssht! Roger that, I'm on my way, Olivia."

"The astronauts must be out fixing something," Naya said.

The children peered out of the window in case they could see the astronauts at work, but there was just the crumbly grey, barren surface of the moon.

"Wait, what's that?" Ashwin leaned closer to the window and Jo joined him. Out across the craters of the moon, a tiny, gold, glowing door appeared.

"There's a door home!" Ashwin shouted.

"That must be where Eddie went!" Jo leapt over to the spacesuits. "Let's go!"

"Maybe we should wait for the astronauts to get back," Naya said. "We could ask them for help."

"Who knows how long they'll be?" Jo grabbed a suit. "Or what kind of trouble Eddie could get into?"

"And haven't you ever wanted to go on a space expedition?" Ashwin held a helmet towards Naya.

Naya reluctantly took the helmet. "There's no atmosphere out there – no air, no warmth and no gravity. No, I've never wanted to go to space." Naya trailed off, looking thoughtful.

ACT IT OUT!

Ashwin and Jo hurriedly put on their suits.

Sound effect: Loud space soundscape, which fades slowly out

Ashwin: Where does this bit go?

Jo: Don't space boots have laces?

Naya: Oh … hang on! Wait for me to get a suit on, too.

Sound effect: Equipment beeps softly around them

Naya: Let me check that you've got your suits on properly. It's dangerous out there.

Ashwin: Thanks, Naya. Maybe being scared is useful sometimes.

Jo: Maybe she's not scared. Maybe she's careful.

Naya: *(Finishes her checks.)* Maybe I am.

Ashwin: We have to go into the airlock before the door to the outside will open.

Sound effect: The airlock opens

Jo: And close the door.

Sound effect: The airlock closes

Jo: Let's do this!

The children step out on to the moon.

5 The Robot

The airlock slid shut behind them and the children set off towards the distant door. Walking on the moon was strange. Naya felt a bit like a kite. Her heavy space boots kept her on the surface, but every long, bouncy step felt like she could float away.

"Wow!" Ashwin's voice sounded funny coming out of the speakers in the helmet. "We're really here. We're on the moon."

Naya paused to look back at the spaceship and gasped. The bottom of the ship was made out of a gigantic whiteboard, which slanted up to join the big rectangular window. The whiteboard displayed a row of silver birch trees.

"Look," Naya said, but as the others turned round, the trees vanished. "It's a whiteboard again."

"Oh! And look up there!" Jo pointed up. "Is that a teacher's desk?"

Floating above the spaceship was the teacher's desk from Year 5. Naya could even see the horse statue that Mr Khan had shown them in assembly.

"It's Mr Khan's desk from Class 5K," Naya said. "Do you remember what their display was about?"

"The moon?" Ashwin bounced along beside her.

"And what about our class?" Naya asked.

"The jungle!" Jo was out in front, leaping as fast as she could towards the door.

"The displays have come to life?" Ashwin gasped.

"Exactly," Naya replied, feeling warm with pride. Maybe she could handle being in space after all.

"I didn't think our school was magic," Jo said. "Just old and a bit smelly."

"Don't be rude about the school!" Naya cried. "It's already got us on the moon."

Beep! A grey cloud was approaching them. Naya floated up to see if she could get a better look, but all she could see was the trail of floating dust. **Beep!**

"Maybe it's the astronauts," Naya said, as she floated back down. Maybe it was even a teacher.

"It looks too small to be a space buggy," Ashwin said.

"But if it's not a space buggy," Jo said, "what else could it be?"

"It's coming straight for us." Naya squinted into the cloud of grey. She could make out something brown and box-like. Then, her heart gave a hard thump as she spotted a glimmer of red. "Killer space robot – from 5K's display!" she cried.

"Killer space robot?!" Ashwin yelled.

"Run!" Jo shouted. But as hard as they tried, running in their spacesuits was almost impossible. The robot was gaining on them. ***Beep!***

The crumbly grey ground shook as the robot rolled to a stop in front of them. Naya frowned. It didn't look like a killer robot. It looked like a kitchen cupboard on wheels, with a long silver neck and a panel with a pair of red eyes. Something that looked a lot like a red and white tea towel was knotted around its neck, the way someone would wear a tie.

ACT IT OUT!

Sound effect: An asteroid passes over the children

Robot: Meep! Identify.

Ashwin: Um.

Robot: Meep! 'Um' not recognised.

Naya: Why don't you tell us who you are?

Robot: Meep! Affirmative! I am Nasabot 1089 Moonbaker.

Jo: Moonbaker?

Robot: Meep! Affirmative! I am searching for ingredients to bake cookies in space.

Naya: Have you found any?

Robot: Meep! *(Sadly)* Negative. All I have found are rocks and star dust.

Jo: Have you seen a little boy?

Robot: Meep! Affirmative! The small male humanoid known as E.D.D.I.E.

Jo: You've seen Eddie!

Naya: Where is he now?

Robot: Meep! E.D.D.I.E. requested assistance to reach Reception.

Jo: Can you help us get to Reception too?

Robot: Meep! Affirmative! Follow me!

The children bounced along after Moonbaker. Naya felt even lighter knowing that Eddie was okay. She couldn't imagine how Jo must feel.

"Meep!" Moonbaker slowed for a moment. "If you look to your right, you will see the Sea of Serenity, which is visible from Earth."

"It's silly to call something a sea when there's no water," Jo said.

"Meep! Affirmative. There is also no flour, butter, eggs, sugar or chocolate chips."

Naya glanced over at Ashwin, who was looking at Moonbaker with a frown on his face. Maybe they should tell Moonbaker that there was no chance it would find baking ingredients on the moon.

The tiny door they had spotted from the spaceship was now big enough to see properly. It looked just like the door to their classroom, and the one behind the waterfall, but this time moon mountains rose behind the door, and it glowed gold around the edges.

"Meep! You have reached your destination!"

Something bumped gently into her glove, and Naya was surprised to see Ashwin trying to take her hand. He jerked his head at Moonbaker. She realised he was asking her, without words, if they should tell Moonbaker about the moon's lack of ingredients. Naya's eyes widened and she nodded, hiding a smile. Ashwin never normally asked Naya for her opinion.

Naya bounced over to the robot. "Moonbaker, I'm sorry, but there aren't any baking ingredients on the moon."

Raised eyebrows appeared on Moonbaker's screen. "Meep! No ingredients? You are certain?"

"We are. It's just more of what you've already found. Rocks and stardust," Naya replied.

"Meep! Processing ..." Moonbaker spun in a little circle. "Meep! My mission is complete. I must report my findings to NASA. Meep! Goodbye, children."

Without another word, Moonbaker rocketed back towards the ship, leaving a trail of grey dust behind him. There was no time to miss the funny little robot. Jo's hand was already on the door handle.

"Let's find Eddie," she said.

6 Candyland

The Mystery Sound

This is the Mystery Sound of Candyland. You will need it later:

- **Three stamps**
- **A yawn**

Experiment with the Mystery Sound:

- **Try it softly and loudly**
- **Try it slow and fast**

Play with your soundscape to see what you like and look out for the sound effects in the **ACT IT OUT!** sections.

After the grey of the moon, the rainbow buildings in front of Ashwin made his eyes hurt. As he took off his helmet, a sweet and buttery smell filled his nostrils.

"Where are we now?" asked Jo.

"What was Reception's display about?" Naya tried to fold her spacesuit, gave up, and discarded it on the brown cobbled road.

"Fairytales," replied Ashwin.

He crossed the road to get a closer look at one of the houses. Its wall was split into square quarters, coloured light pink and light yellow, and it was spongey under his fingers. "Is this made of cake?"

"Cake?" Jo joined him. "Why would there be houses made of cake?"

"Hansel and Gretel," Naya said. "Look down there, that house is made of gingerbread!"

"Moonbaker would have loved it here," Ashwin replied. "What do you think, head down that road towards the town square, or …" Ashwin's stomach gurgled "… stop for a very quick snack?"

"I am a bit hungry," Naya admitted.

"We do need our energy to find Eddie," Jo agreed, edging towards the house. "Maybe we could have a little five-minute break?"

"Okay then …" Ashwin looked at Naya, Naya looked at Jo, and then all three rushed to the house to devour handfuls of cake.

"Yum! This place is like Candyland!" Naya said, with her mouth full. "What's the windowsill made out of, Ashwin?"

"Chocolate fingers." Ashwin handed her some. He was glad she seemed less angry at him. Candyland was making everyone feel better. Even Jo was smiling.

"I think Eddie stopped here, too." Jo pointed at some bite marks lower down the wall.

Someone coughed loudly behind the children. "Ahem!"

They stopped eating and turned slowly around. Standing on the road were two grown-ups, with their arms crossed and their mouths turned down into frowns. They looked just like pictures they'd seen in story books of Hansel and Gretel, but larger and angrier.

ACT IT OUT!

Sound effect: *(Quietly)* **The mystery sound** *(stamp, stamp, stamp, yawn)*

Gretel: We had reports of someone eating our brand-new housing estate.

Hansel: And it is obviously you.

Naya: We're sorry, we didn't think anyone would be living here.

Gretel: Do you think we build houses for fun?

Ashwin: We can fix them.

Jo: We're searching for Eddie, have you seen him?

Gretel: No, but if we find him, we'll put him in prison too.

Naya: Prison?

Hansel and Gretel put handcuffs on the children and lead them towards the town square.

Jo: You can't put us in prison! We need to find my little brother and get home.

Gretel: Don't worry, you won't be in prison for long.

Hansel: We're going to get the judge.

Gretel: And because you ate our homes ...

Hansel: ... He'll most certainly eat you!

They lock the children in a prison cell and leave.

Naya: That's not what judges do!

Sound effect: *(Quietly)* **The mystery sound**

Ashwin: Come back!
(To Naya and Jo) I always thought Hansel and Gretel would be nicer.

Naya: They said the judge was going to eat us. Eat us!

Jo: These bars are made of metal. We can't even nibble our way out. Eddie must be so frightened out there all on his own. Why did we eat that cake?

Sound effect: *(Quietly)* **The mystery sound**

Ashwin: I'm sorry! It's all my fault. I have the worst ideas and, Naya, you were right, I never listen.

Naya: But, I'm sorry too. I *am* scared lots of the time and you *do* have good ideas. Maybe we need to learn how to work together again.

Sound effect: *(Quietly)* **The mystery sound**

Naya: Did you hear that?

Jo: And I'm sorry as well. If only I'd been a better sister, maybe we wouldn't have had to chase Eddie down a waterfall and across the moon. He's my little brother and I love him, but I was always so mean to him.

Eddie: That's okay, Jo, I love you too.

Ashwin, Naya and Jo: EDDIE!

Eddie appears on the other side of the bars.

Jo: Oh, my goodness. Eddie! Are you all right? I was so worried. Are you hurt? What happened to you?

Eddie: I met a robot on the moon!

Ashwin: Us too.

Eddie: And ate a bit of a house.

Naya: Yep.

Eddie: And found the key to your cell hanging on the wall.

Ashwin, Naya and Jo: YAY!

Eddie releases them and they all hug him.

Jo: Now, hold my hand and don't let go until we get out of Candyland. I'm going to look after you.

Naya: Why didn't you wait for us, Eddie?

Eddie: I was going to come and find you, but I wanted to get the school door key that my teacher keeps in her desk first.

Ashwin: Your teacher has a key?

Eddie: I did try to tell you. But now I've found my classroom, I can't find her desk.

Ashwin: Hmmmm. Okay. Who's got any ideas?

Naya: I do. We saw the whiteboard and the teacher's desks in space and in the jungle. They were near the door, just like in our real classrooms.

Jo: But that's not what Reception looks like. They have their whiteboard on the other side of the room.

Ashwin: So, we need to get to the other side of Candyland, look for the whiteboard and the teacher's desk, and grab that key.

Sound effect: *(Louder)* **The mystery sound**

Naya: And we should do it fast. Whatever is making that noise is getting closer.

Ashwin: Okay, team, let's go!

7 The Key

The sun was setting over the red cherry roofs of Candyland as the children sprinted out of the prison. That strange noise was getting closer. Naya could feel it in her bones.

Stamp, stamp, stamp, yawn.

What could be making a sound like that?

"We need to go deeper into Candyland to find the desk. Shall we follow the road?" Jo asked.

The cobbled road led down a shadowy alley where the dark houses leaned in and blocked out the last of the daylight. Shivering, Naya fought back the urge to run. She clenched her fists and stepped forwards.

"Let's go," she said.

The entrance to the alley was big enough for the children to fit through side-by-side, but the road swiftly narrowed until they were walking in a line. They inched between the crooked buildings, and Naya tried to ignore the inky shadows growing around them. The dark seemed almost endless.

"Maybe we should go back ..." Naya trailed off. "Oh! Wait!" She squinted and sighed with relief. There was a faint glimmer of light ahead.

Naya squeezed out of the alley – and saw the whiteboard! It was baked into the side of a tall biscuit building, and on it was a line of silver birch trees.

"The trees again," she gasped.

"The whiteboard!" Ashwin caught up with her. "What did you say about trees?"

The trees were gone, but Naya was used to this by now. "Never mind," she said. "The desk in the jungle was in the same tree as the whiteboard."

"And the desk in space was floating above it," Jo added, holding Eddie's hand.

"So maybe the desk is inside the building?" Naya concluded.

Ashwin ran up to the door. "It's locked." He smiled at them. "But it's made of chocolate ..."

A few moments later, Naya's hands were sticky, and she felt far too full, but they were in the vast entrance hall of the building. She flicked on a switch and dull orange lights buzzed on around them. Apart from a dusty toolbox, the hall was empty.

"Hansel and Gretel aren't going to be happy about that door," Naya said.

Stamp, stamp, stamp, yawn.

The children froze and Naya shivered as a fearsome thought crept into her head.

"That's not the judge that Hansel and Gretel sent to eat us ... is it?" she whispered.

Stamp, stamp, stamp, yawn.

"It's getting closer!" Ashwin yelled. "Quick! Search downstairs!"

The children scattered. A moment later, they were back in the entrance hall, wide-eyed and shaking their heads. For once, everyone looked as terrified as Naya felt. There was no sign of the desk and they were running out of time. The judge was coming.

"Let's go upstairs!" Naya cried. "Stay together!"

Stamp, stamp, stamp, yawn.

The children rushed up a staircase and skidded to a stop by a wide window. The alley that they had just walked down was shaking.

Stamp, stamp, stamp, crash!

"Hide!" As Naya pulled the others down and out of sight, she caught a glimpse of a huge figure crashing out of the alley and stumbling to a stop, surrounded by debris. The children cautiously peeked over the windowsill. The creature was enormous, with knobbly grey skin, glowing yellow eyes and arms as thick as tree trunks.

"Is that a troll?" Eddie whispered.

Suddenly, as if it had remembered its mission, the troll raised its arms and snarled. It stomped forwards three times making the ground shake. Naya gasped, but then the troll stopped. It yawned and scratched its head.

ACT IT OUT!

Sound effect: *(Quietly)* **The mystery sound**

Ashwin: It's coming! Quick, we've got to find the desk.

Jo: There are so many rooms.

Naya: But that shambling troll isn't going anywhere fast. We can do this.

Eddie: You're so brave, Naya.

Jo: Everyone, split up. Eddie, stay with me and hold my hand.

Ashwin: Let's go!

The children scatter to check different rooms.

Sound effect: *(Louder)* **The mystery sound**

Jo: The troll is in the building!

Naya: No desk in my room.

Jo: There's nothing in ours either.

The children meet in the corridor.

Ashwin: Check further down the corridor.

Sound effect: *(Louder)* **The mystery sound**

Naya: It's coming up the stairs.

Ashwin: Go!

The children dart into different rooms.

Jo: We'll check in this room.

Sound effect: *(Louder)* **The mystery sound**

Eddie: It's here! It's here!

Ashwin: The troll?

Eddie: No, the desk!

Ashwin joins Eddie and Jo at the teacher's desk.
Naya stays by the door to watch for the troll.

Naya: *(Whispers)* It's searching the rooms – it doesn't
             know where we are. Everybody, be quiet.

Jo: *(Quietly)* Where does your teacher keep the
             key, Eddie?

Eddie: *(Loudly)* In her drawer.

Naya, Ashwin and Jo: Shhh!

Sound effect: *(Loudly)* **The mystery sound**

Naya: It's coming! Find the key.

Eddie opens a desk drawer.

Eddie: It's in here!

Ashwin: It's glowing.

Jo: It's shaking.

Eddie grabs the key.

Eddie: It's hot.

Sound effect: *(Loudly)* **The mystery sound**

Naya rushes over.

Naya: The troll is here!

The room transforms around them.

Ashwin: What's happening?

Jo: The room is changing!

Naya: Everyone, hold hands.

The children hold hands. The floor shakes, they wobble and all fall over. They are no longer in Candyland. They are back in the corridor by the school's big red front door.

Ashwin: Are we back?

Naya: I think so.

Jo: Did the troll come with us?

Everyone stops to listen. Just then, Eddie yawns loudly, sounding just like the troll. The others jump in fright.

Eddie: Sorry, I'm tired.

Jo: Don't worry, we'll be home soon.

Ashwin: We're right by the front door. Should we open it?

Naya: Yes, let's do it.

Everyone looked at the glowing key. There was a chance that they would open the door and be on a volcano, or under the sea, or anywhere at all, but Naya held out her hand.

"I'll do it," she said.

The key was still warm and, as she slid it into the lock, it was like everything clicked into place. Jo had realised how important Eddie was to her. Ashwin had learnt to listen. Naya would have never volunteered to open the door before, but after running through the jungle, bouncing across the moon, and escaping from Candyland, she felt ready for anything.

The red door creaked open, and sunshine flooded into the corridor. The last of the children and parents were still wandering down the path away from the school.

"I thought we were gone for hours," Jo said.

"It's magic, Jo," Eddie said, as if that explained everything.

"What next, team?" Ashwin asked.

"Home for some snacks?" Naya suggested.

"Home for some snacks!" they all agreed, without hesitation.

Naya left the key on the doormat inside the school, and pulled the door closed with a bang. Ashwin, Jo and Eddie were already on their way down the path, and Naya walked slowly past the silver birches next to the door. They shone at her, like they had on the whiteboards, and somehow it felt like a wink.

"Wait for me!" Naya ran after her friends. The trees were beautiful and mysterious, but she'd had enough adventure for one day. It was time to go home.

The End

Now answer the questions ...

1 What does 'deciduous' mean?

2 What class are Naya, Jo and Ashwin in?

3 What happened when Eddie tried to cross the river?

4 On page 27, Jo 'clenched her fists tightly by her side'. What does this say about how she is feeling?

5 What did you think would happen when they went out on to the moon?

6 On page 48, it says: 'The dark seemed almost endless.' How did the author's choice of phrase to describe the dark add to the meaning?

7 What was Ashwin's character like at the end of the story compared to the beginning?

8 Have you had an adventure with your friends or family that changed you for the better? What happened?